the Solar System

Author Sophie Allan
Illustrator Dawn Cooper
Subject Consultant Josh Barker

Project Editor Clare Lloyd
Project Art Editor Charlotte Jennings
Editor Lizzie Munsey
Designer Sadie Thomas
Jacket Designer Charlotte Jennings
Jacket Co-ordinator Magda Pszuk
Senior Picture Researcher Sakshi Saluja
Producer, Pre-Production Becky Fallowfield
Producer Magdalena Bojko
Managing Editor Penny Smith
Deputy Art Director Mabel Chan
Publishing Director Sarah Larter

First published in Great Britain in 2023 by
Dorling Kindersley Limited
DK, One Embassy Gardens, 8 Viaduct Gardens,
London, SW11 7BW

The authorised representative in the
EEA is Dorling Kindersley Verlag GmbH.
Arnulfstr. 124, 80636 Munich, Germany

A CIP catalogue record for this book
is available from the British Library.
ISBN: 978-0-2416-3129-4

Printed and bound in China

www.dk.com

This book was made with Forest
Stewardship Council™ certified paper –
one small step in DK's commitment to a
sustainable future. For more information
go to www.dk.com/our-green-pledge

Contents

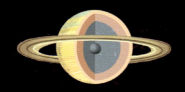

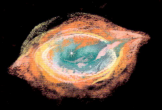

WELCOME TO THE SOLAR SYSTEM

The Solar System is the name of our home area in space. We share it with seven other planets, as well as with many other incredible celestial objects.

Earth and the other planets move around the Sun in a constant dance, held in place by an invisible force called gravity. For thousands of years, humans have been on a quest to discover and understand more about our space neighbourhood. We once made up stories to explain what we saw. We have used mathematics and telescopes to understand and predict how the Solar System works. More recently, we have sent a small army of spacecraft out into space, to study and explore the planets, moons, and other objects we find out there.

! Never look directly at the Sun

There are four rocky planets...

The Sun

Mercury

Venus

Earth

Mars

The Solar System is made up of the Sun, eight planets, dwarf planets, moons, asteroids, and comets.

In this book, we explore the strange and wonderful objects that make up our Solar System, starting with its powerhouse, the Sun.

We see how our understanding of the Solar System has grown, from space stories told by early civilizations to space missions that are revolutionizing our understanding of our neighbours. We discover how the Solar System formed, how it has changed over time, and what the future holds for it and us. We look at where we will go next, and where we might find life if it exists outside of our planet.

Most importantly, we see what a unique and special place Earth is. So, what are you waiting for? Buckle up, turn the page, and uncover the mysteries of space for yourself!

...two gas giants...

...and two ice giants.

Jupiter

Saturn

Uranus

Neptune

CHAPTER 1

UP IN SPACE

Early humans were fascinated by what they could see in the night sky.
They came up with incredible stories to explain what they could see.

Science has come a long way since our early ideas about space.
Now we have telescopes so scientists can look into space more
clearly and make observations. Their findings allow us to
understand the structure of our Solar System, and how it works.
We now understand how the Solar System formed, and how
our star, the Sun, compares to other stars.

Black hole

In the centre of the Milky Way sits Sagittarius A*, a supermassive black hole. A black hole is an extremely dense place in space, which light cannot escape from. In May 2022, astronomers released the first image of a black hole. It shows the radio waves around Sagittarius A*.

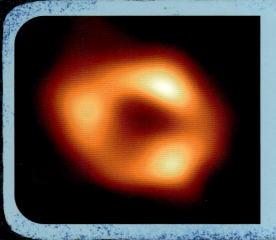

Spiral arms

Our Solar System is inside the Orion arm of the Milky Way. The other arms of our galaxy can sometimes be seen as bands of stars across the sky, like in this picture. They are only visible at certain times of year and on clear nights, far away from city lights.

Our place in space

Space is unimaginably big. It contains more stars than there are grains of sand on all the beaches on Earth! These stars are not evenly spread out – they clump together in groups of hundreds of billions, called galaxies. Each galaxy is a collection of stars, gas, and dust, held together by a force called gravity. Earth is a small part of our Solar System, which is a tiny part of a huge, spiral-shaped galaxy called the Milky Way.

Planet Earth is here

Types of galaxies

Galaxies are grouped into three main types: spiral, elliptical, and irregular. Our Universe contains hundreds of billions of them! Astronomers believe that, like the Milky Way, most large galaxies have a black hole at their centre.

Bar of stars

Spiral

These galaxies are wide, flat disks with spinning arms of gas, dust, and stars. Barred spiral galaxies like the Milky Way have a bar of stars running through the centre.

Elliptical

These galaxies are oval-shaped and look fairly uniform, with no spiral arm structure. They are made up of older stars.

Irregular

As the name suggests, these galaxies have no regular shape and often look very chaotic! They tend to be small, with lots of gas, dust, and young stars.

Our galaxy, the Milky Way

Star stories

Humans have huge imaginations and a desire to make sense of what we see. For thousands of years, people around the world have looked up at the Sun, Moon, stars, and planets, and created stories to explain them. Many of these are linked to ideas about gods, goddesses, religions, and sacred tales.

Chasing the Sun

In traditional Inuit stories, the Sun and the Moon are sister and brother. One day, they disagreed. Malina (the Sun) ran away and her brother, Igaluk (the Moon) chased after her. This is why the Sun and Moon move across the sky.

It began with an egg

In traditional Chinese Daoist stories, everything began in chaos. Out of the chaos came an egg. Out of the egg burst Pangu, the first being. Pangu separated the heavens from the Earth, carved Earth's features, and created stars in the sky.

Naming the planets

The ancient Romans named the planets they could see after their five most famous gods. When telescopes were invented and more planets were recorded, these were also named after gods.

Mercury

This planet races across the night sky at great speed. It is named after the god of travellers, traders, and tricksters.

Venus

The brightest planet in the night sky is named after Venus, the goddess of love, beauty, and prosperity.

Mars

Mars is the red planet. Its colour is linked to anger and bloodshed, so it is named after the god of war.

Jupiter

The biggest planet of them all is named after Jupiter, king of the gods.

Protecting the family

In Egyptian myths, Shu (god of air) and Tefnut (god of moisture) had two children: a son named Geb and a daughter named Nut. Geb lay down and became god of the Earth. Nut protected her brother, becoming goddess of the stars.

Neptune

Neptune was first sighted in 1846 by Johann Galle. It is named after the Roman god of the sea.

Uranus

First sighted in 1781 by the astronomer William Herschel, Uranus is named after the Greek god of the sky.

Saturn

Saturn is named after the god of agriculture and wealth, who is also Jupiter's father.

Studying the skies

Astronomers have observed the sky for thousands of years. Studying the movement of the planets and stars allowed them to model our Solar System. As our understanding of maths and science improved, so did the models. The invention of telescopes helped astronomers to confirm new ideas, but they weren't always accepted straight away.

Earth at the centre

Early models of our Solar System put the Earth at the centre of everything. Nearly 2,000 years ago, an astronomer named Ptolemy used his observations of the Moon and the planets to confirm what most already believed: that they orbited (travelled around) the Earth. This model is known as the geocentric (Earth-centred) model.

Uranus and Neptune didn't appear in early models of the Solar System, because they hadn't been discovered yet!

Saturn
Venus
Earth
Mercury
Sun
Moon
Jupiter
Mars

PTOLEMY

Wandering stars

From the Earth, astronomers such as Ptolemy observed five moving "stars" that seemed to wander across the sky. They named these objects planets, from the Ancient Greek word "planetes", which means "wanderer". The planets they identified were Mercury, Venus, Mars, Jupiter, and Saturn.

Sun at the centre

In 1543, Polish astronomer Nicolaus Copernicus used his observations to explain why the stars seemed to move in the night sky. He suggested this was because the planets orbited the Sun, in a "heliocentric" model. Modern science has proved that Copernicus was correct – the planets do orbit the Sun.

COPERNICUS

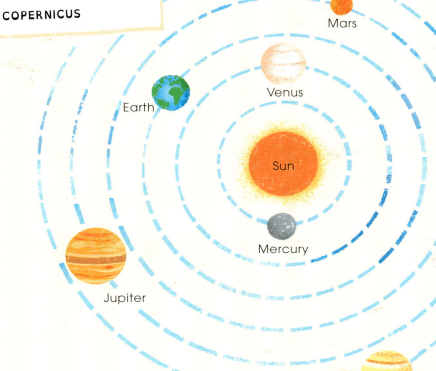

Mars

Venus

Earth

Sun

Mercury

Jupiter

Saturn

"Heliocentric" comes from the Greek word "helios", which means "Sun".

Unpopular truth

Once the telescope was invented in the early 1600s, astronomers were able to make much better observations of the stars and planets. In 1632, Italian astronomer Galileo Galilei published a book supporting Copernicus' Sun-centred theory. This went against the view of the Catholic Church at the time: that the Earth was the centre of the Solar System. Galileo was ordered to stay at home for the rest of his life.

This swirling disk of dust is called the solar nebula.

The Sun

1 In the beginning

The formation of the Solar System began when a gigantic cloud of dust and gas started to collapse. As the cloud collapsed, it spun faster and faster, forming a dense, flat disk shape.

Some of the lightest gases were spun right out to the cold, outer edge of the disk.

The birth of our Solar System

Planet Earth is just a small part of a network of planets, moons, asteroids, and comets that move around the Sun, called the Solar System. But how did the Solar System begin? The answer lies in an event that happened around 4.6 billion years ago...

Small, leftover pieces of material became asteroids, comets, and dwarf planets.

2

Birth of a star

The enormous cloud collapsed due to the force of gravity, and the centre became hotter and hotter until it began to fuse (combine) hydrogen atoms to produce helium. This released a huge amount of energy, creating a shining star – the Sun.

More than 99 per cent of the material from the dust cloud went into the Sun.

3

The Solar System

The leftover material from the cloud began to clump together, forming planets around the Sun. The material closest to the Sun formed the rocky planets. Further away from the Sun, cooler gases formed enormous gas giants (planets that are mostly made of hydrogen and helium gases).

Our Solar System

Our understanding of our Solar System has grown over time. Today, we have a clear idea of what our Solar System looks like, thanks to high-powered telescopes and space exploration. The fiery Sun sits in the centre of the Solar System. Held in its orbit are planets, dwarf planets, and thousands of asteroids and comets.

Closest to the Sun are four rocky planets: Mercury, Venus, Earth, and Mars.

Comets are balls of rock and ice that orbit the Sun.

MERCURY

MARS

EARTH

Asteroids

URANUS

JUPITER

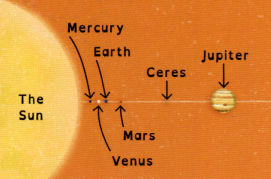

Asteroid Belt

Asteroids are rocky objects that travel around the Sun. Millions of them orbit between Mars and Jupiter, in an area known as the Asteroid Belt.

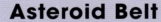

The Sun

Mercury

Earth

Mars

Venus

Ceres

Jupiter

Saturn

Uranus

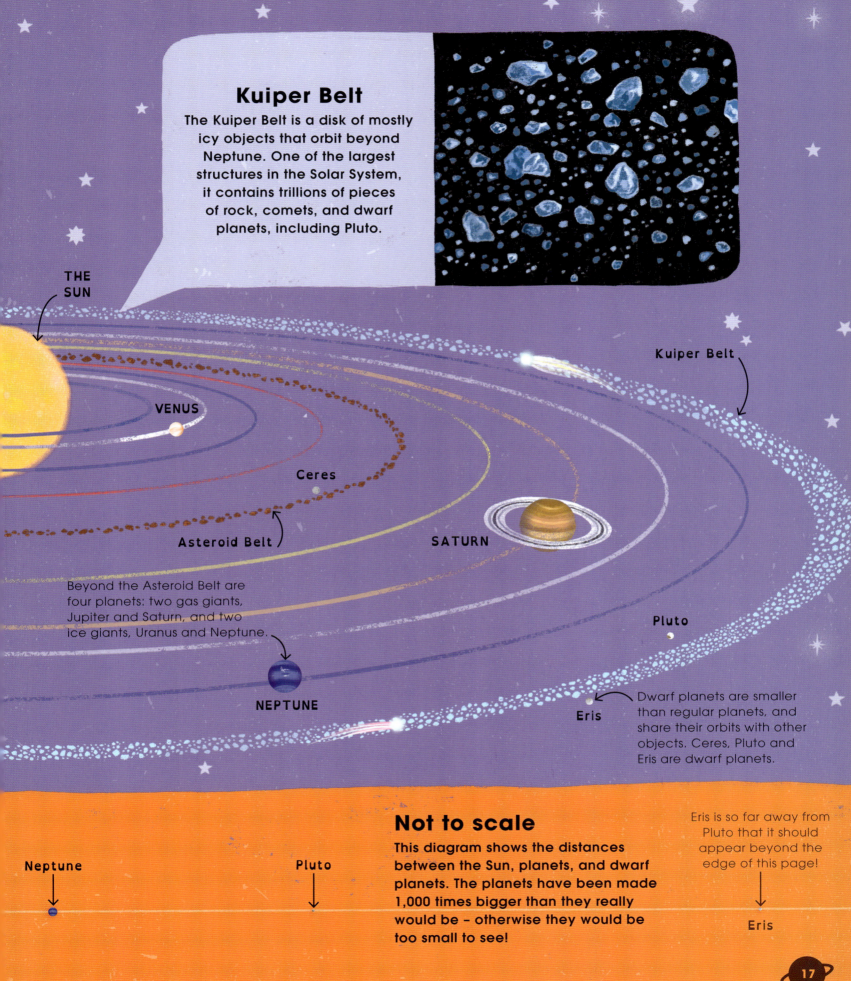

Kuiper Belt

The Kuiper Belt is a disk of mostly icy objects that orbit beyond Neptune. One of the largest structures in the Solar System, it contains trillions of pieces of rock, comets, and dwarf planets, including Pluto.

THE SUN

Kuiper Belt

VENUS

Ceres

Asteroid Belt

SATURN

Beyond the Asteroid Belt are four planets: two gas giants, Jupiter and Saturn, and two ice giants, Uranus and Neptune.

Pluto

NEPTUNE

Eris

Dwarf planets are smaller than regular planets, and share their orbits with other objects. Ceres, Pluto and Eris are dwarf planets.

Not to scale

Neptune

Pluto

This diagram shows the distances between the Sun, planets, and dwarf planets. The planets have been made 1,000 times bigger than they really would be – otherwise they would be too small to see!

Eris is so far away from Pluto that it should appear beyond the edge of this page!

Eris

Our Sun

At the centre of our Solar System lies our local star – the Sun. It contains most of the mass in the Solar System, and its gravity keeps the planets circling around it. The Sun is just one of an unimaginably huge number of stars in the Universe, and in comparison to some it is surprisingly ordinary!

Star colours

Our Sun looks yellow or orange, but a star's colour depends on the temperature of its surface. The hotter stars are blue or white, while cooler stars appear orange or red. The Sun lies in the middle of this star temperature range, at 5,500°C (9,900°F).

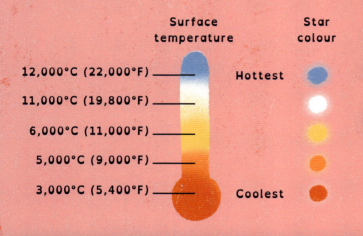

Surface temperature	Star colour
12,000°C (22,000°F)	Hottest
11,000°C (19,800°F)	
6,000°C (11,000°F)	
5,000°C (9,000°F)	
3,000°C (5,400°F)	Coolest

This colourful display of stars was captured by the Hubble Space Telescope.

Star sizes

The Sun is the largest object in the Solar System and 109 times wider than the Earth. But it is only average-sized for a star. Stars that are much bigger than our Sun are called giant stars. Even more enormous stars are called supergiants, and they can be up to 1,500 times wider than the Sun!

The Sun

Sirius

Pollux

Aldebaran

Sirius, Pollux, Aldebaran, and Rigel are giant stars.

Rigel

Betelgeuse

Betelgeuse is a supergiant.

Solar Orbiter

Observing the Sun

You should never look directly at the Sun, but luckily we have spacecraft to observe it for us! The NASA and European Space Agency's Solar and Heliospheric Observatory (SOHO) and Solar Orbiter (SolO) missions have captured the closest-ever images of the Sun. They show that the Sun is constantly throwing out material, in events called solar flares.

This incredibly detailed image of the Sun was captured in March 2022, by the *Solar Orbiter* space probe.

CHAPTER 2

THE ROCKY PLANETS

Earth is our very own ball of rock, metal, and soil. It is unique, but it's not the only rocky planet in our Solar System...

The four planets closest to the Sun are known as the rocky planets. Earth also has its own rocky neighbour – the Moon. Many missions have headed out into space to explore these rocky objects and find out more about them. The other rocky planets are similar to Earth in some ways, and yet they have fascinating differences, too.

Mercury

Mercury is the closest planet to the Sun, and the smallest planet in the Solar System – it is barely bigger than our Moon! It is so small and so close to the heat of the Sun that it can't hold onto an atmosphere like the Earth can. However, this small, rocky planet has many secrets...

Time talk

Mercury is close to the Sun and orbits it very quickly. One year on Mercury is equal to just 88 Earth days.

You would celebrate more than four times as many birthdays if you lived on Mercury rather than Earth!

Mercury spins very slowly compared to Earth. One day on Mercury is 59 Earth days.

Mariner 10 was the first spacecraft to study Mercury.

More to explore

Mercury is the least explored of the rocky planets – only two spacecraft visited it before 2023. Mercury is close to the Sun, which makes it difficult to send spacecrafts there because they could get pulled into the burning Sun by its gravity.

Hot and cold

Mercury spins very slowly and has no atmosphere. This means the side facing the Sun (day side) gets extremely hot, reaching temperatures of around 430°C (806°F).

Craters, craters everywhere

Without an atmosphere to protect it, Mercury's surface is covered in craters. These are impact "scars" created by comets and meteorites crashing into it. Some of these craters are very deep and permanently dark at the bottom. Scientists believe there may be frozen water in the depths of some craters.

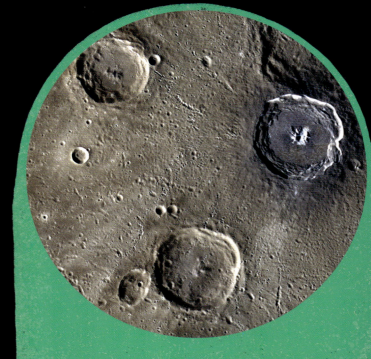

NASA's MESSENGER mission revealed a series of "hollows" on the surface of Mercury. These shallow dents are surrounded by bright, reflective material. The features are very young, and scientists are keen to learn more about how they form.

BepiColombo mission

In 2018, The European Space Agency teamed up with The Japan Aerospace Exploration Agency to launch the *BepiColombo* on a 7-year journey to explore Mercury. Two spacecraft aim to orbit the planet. They carry high-tech equipment, which should help them learn about the planet's surface features, magnetic field, water ice, and more.

BepiColombo spacecraft

In contrast, the side facing away from the Sun (night side) is a freezing –180°C (–292°F). Your best chance of survival on Mercury would be to move with the terminator – the line between the day and night sides of the planet.

Venus

Venus is the hottest of the planets, even though Mercury is closer to the Sun. It is nearly the same size as Earth, with a hot, thick, acidic atmosphere and extremely high pressure (force of air pushing on an object) at the surface. The conditions on Venus make it incredibly difficult to explore, but learning about the planet could be vital to understanding more about our own planet.

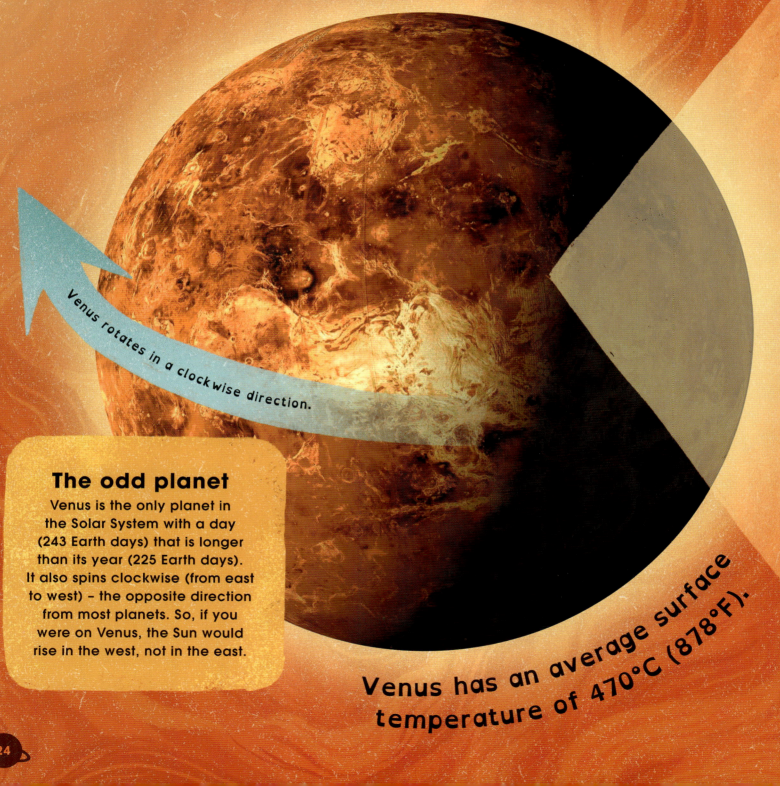

Venus rotates in a clockwise direction.

The odd planet

Venus is the only planet in the Solar System with a day (243 Earth days) that is longer than its year (225 Earth days). It also spins clockwise (from east to west) – the opposite direction from most planets. So, if you were on Venus, the Sun would rise in the west, not in the east.

Venus has an average surface temperature of 470°C (878°F).

The ultimate greenhouse

Venus has a thick atmosphere made up mainly of carbon dioxide gas. Incoming light from the Sun is absorbed by the surface of Venus and then radiated (sent out) as heat. The carbon dioxide reflects and traps this heat, warming Venus. This greenhouse effect is what makes Venus so hot.

Under pressure

The thick atmosphere on Venus means air pressure at its surface is about 90 times greater than on the surface of Earth. This pressure, extreme heat, and acid rain make it difficult for spacecraft to survive. The record so far is held by the *Venera 13* probe, which lasted just over 2 hours.

Behind the cloud

We can't see through the atmosphere and clouds of Venus, but there are other ways to study it. Spacecraft such as NASA's *Magellan* have used radar to "look" through the clouds. We now know that the surface of Venus is dry and rocky, with mountains and volcanoes.

Venera 13 probe

A watery past?

The European Space Agency's Venus Express mission arrived at Venus in April 2006. It has sent back a huge amount of information about Venus's atmosphere and climate. One major finding was that the planet was losing oxygen and hydrogen, which make up water. This suggests that Venus may have had a lot more water in the past.

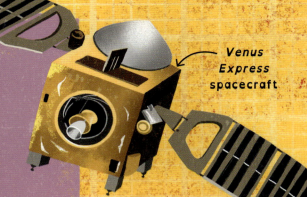

Venus Express spacecraft

Venus vs Earth

VENUS

Venus has a lot in common with Earth. They are similar sizes, and the layers of the planets are very alike: each has an iron core beneath a rocky layer, called the mantle. Venus also has volcanoes, like Earth. Scientists are interested in finding out why Venus ended up being so different to Earth, and are planning to send spacecraft to the planet.

Solid inner core

Liquid outer core

Mantle

Crust

EARTH

Solid inner core

Liquid outer core

Mantle

Crust

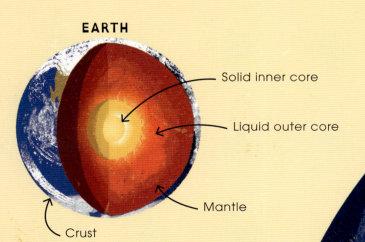

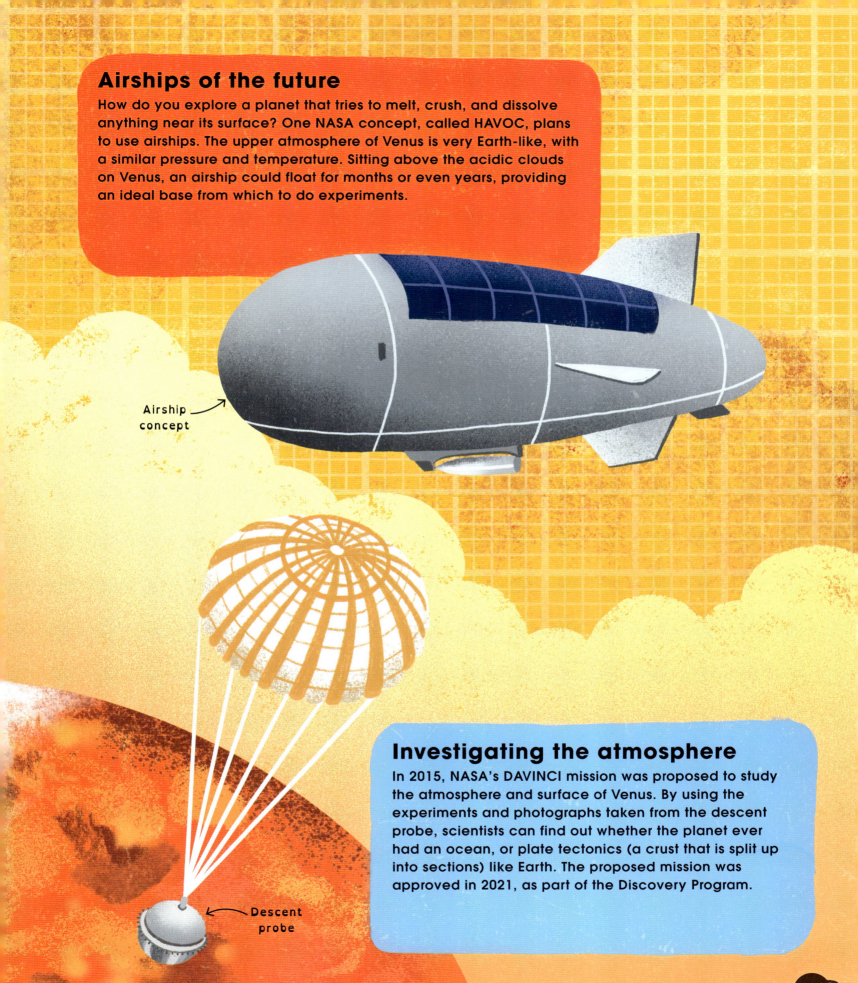

Airships of the future

How do you explore a planet that tries to melt, crush, and dissolve anything near its surface? One NASA concept, called HAVOC, plans to use airships. The upper atmosphere of Venus is very Earth-like, with a similar pressure and temperature. Sitting above the acidic clouds on Venus, an airship could float for months or even years, providing an ideal base from which to do experiments.

Airship concept

Investigating the atmosphere

In 2015, NASA's DAVINCI mission was proposed to study the atmosphere and surface of Venus. By using the experiments and photographs taken from the descent probe, scientists can find out whether the planet ever had an ocean, or plate tectonics (a crust that is split up into sections) like Earth. The proposed mission was approved in 2021, as part of the Discovery Program.

Descent probe

The Earth through time

Our planet has come a long way from the collapsing cloud of dust and gas from which it began. The early days of Earth were hot and inhospitable to life. Slowly, as things cooled down, it became the unique blue marble we treasure today. Let's look at a few of Earth's early milestones...

1 The Earth is "born"

The Earth formed around 4.5 billion years ago, in a collapsing disc of dust and gas around the Sun. As bits of rock clumped together they gained gravity, pulling more small pieces of rock and dust towards them. As Earth got bigger, its gravity got stronger, pulling all the rock towards the centre, and causing Earth to get very hot.

2 Melted rock

The young Earth was so hot that all of the rock and metal inside it melted and mixed together, becoming a giant ball of magma. As the magma began to cool, denser material such as iron and nickel (metals) began to sink towards the centre, to form the Earth's core. Less dense materials formed a layer above the core, called the mantle.

Boom

3 The Moon

About 4.45 billion years ago, a large asteroid hit Earth. This sent a large amount of material off into space, which then became the Moon.

4 Asteroid attack

At the same time that the Moon formed, asteroids (space rocks) constantly smashed into the Earth. The asteroids melted and became part of the Earth, releasing the water they were carrying into the atmosphere as steam. This water became very important to our planet.

5 Our atmosphere

About 4 billion years ago, Earth cooled down enough for its surface to solidify into a crust. The steam from asteroid impacts became liquid, forming our first seas. Earth was an inhospitable place, with large volcanoes shooting gases up from below the crust. These gases formed our atmosphere, keeping heat in as the planet's surface slowly cooled.

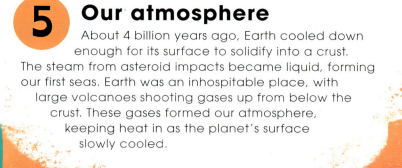

6 Simple life

About 3.8 billion years ago, the first cells (the smallest building blocks of all living things) emerged. They were very simple – it would be a long time before more complex life came along.

7 Our first ice age

Just over 2 billion years ago our planet got extremely cold. Scientists believe this was because there were not enough greenhouse gases in the atmosphere to trap heat. The entire surface of the Earth froze, in the first of a series of "ice ages".

8 Life on Earth

Over time, Earth's simple cells evolved into more complicated ones, which grouped together to form larger living things. Shelled creatures and fish evolved into the great dinosaurs. However, 65 million years ago a huge asteroid impact wiped out three-quarters of life on Earth. Small mammals were among those that survived, leading to the age we live in now – the age of mammals.

The Earth as it appears today.

Not too hot, not too cold

Our Sun releases energy in the form of light and heat. Planets that are close to the Sun, such as Mercury and Venus, are so hot that liquid water would quickly boil away. Gas giants, such as Jupiter, are cold and so far from the Sun that liquid water would instantly freeze. Liquid water can only exist in a small range of distances from the Sun. We call this area the habitable zone, or the Goldilocks zone.

The Goldilocks planet

The Earth is unique within our Solar System for many reasons. It is the only place in the entire Universe where we know that life exists, and it is Earth's unique features that allow life to flourish. It is "just right" for life, which is why it is sometimes called the "Goldilocks" planet.

Goldilocks zone

The Sun

Mercury

Venus

Too hot!

Earth

Mars

Too cold!

A well-balanced atmosphere

Earth sits firmly in the middle of the Goldilocks zone, whilst our neighbours, Venus and Mars, sit to either side of it. The high levels of carbon dioxide in Venus's atmosphere trap heat from the Sun, making the planet far too hot for water to remain on its surface. Mars only has a very thin atmosphere, and is too cold for liquid water. The Earth has just the right amount of carbon dioxide in the atmosphere to keep it warm, but not too hot.

Magnetic magic

Earth is surrounded by an invisible force field, called a magnetic field. It is produced by moving metals in Earth's outer core and mantle. The magnetic field is important because it protects Earth from solar wind – particles that stream outwards from the Sun. Without our magnetic field, the solar wind would strip away Earth's atmosphere.

Mars is further from the Sun and smaller than the Earth. It cooled quickly once it formed, leaving a solid, metal core. As the metal isn't moving, there is no magnetic field to protect it. Over time, the solar wind has blown away Mars' atmosphere, leaving it a cold, dry planet. Scientists believe it was once more Earthlike.

Earth's magnetic field acts like a barrier, protecting our planet.

The Sun releases a constant stream of charged particles, called solar wind.

Earth and auroras

When a solar flare happens, a huge number of charged particles are thrown out into space from the Sun. These squash Earth's magnetic field, causing parts to snap and reconnect. Some solar wind particles travel down the magnetic field to Earth's poles. They interact with the atmosphere there, producing an amazing light show known as an aurora. Earth is not the only planet to have auroras, but we are the only one with people to enjoy them!

In this image from the Hubble Space Telescope, you can see an amazing aurora on Jupiter.

An aurora from Earth

An aurora from the ISS

Auroras from space

Auroras are spectacular from Earth, but they can be even more amazing from space! Astronauts on the International Space Station (ISS), a giant laboratory orbiting the Earth, get an amazing view of auroras – from above.

The Earth from above

Earth is the only planet currently capable of supporting human life, so it is important that we take care of it. Satellite technology allows us to constantly scan the surface of our planet from space, so we can study what is happening and look for changes that might affect us. We use this data to help us predict what may come next.

Satellite armies

Studying Earth from the ground can give us information, but only about a small area at a time. If we want to really study our planet, we need to combine this information with observations from space. Space agencies have armies of satellites looking down on the Earth, gathering information, and sending it to scientists. There are many ways to help and protect our planet by looking at it from space.

Plant problems

We need plants for food and for turning carbon dioxide into oxygen we can breathe. We can see how healthy plants are from space by looking at the amount of near infrared light they reflect. The healthier the plants, the more near infrared we see. Scientists can identify areas where plants are dying and try to work out why.

Wild weather

Extreme weather events can be very dangerous to humans. For example, hurricanes bring destructive winds and heavy rainfall. By studying ocean currents and wind direction from space, we can predict where a hurricane will go next and warn people so they can seek safety.

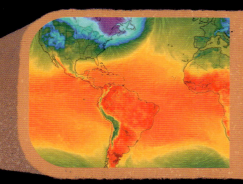

Temperature changes

Our planet is gradually heating up (global warming). The speed at which this is happening has a lot of scientists worried. Using long-term studies of the temperature of our planet and data about different gases, such as carbon dioxide, scientists can try to predict what will happen next.

Disappearing glaciers

As our planet warms up, glaciers (giant stores of frozen water) melt faster than they can refreeze. This increases sea levels, and damages the habitats that many animals depend on for survival. Satellites allow us to monitor these changes and the impact of global warming over time.

Penguin predictions

It is tricky to track penguins in Antarctica, but scientists have found a solution. They have been using satellite images to study penguin poo! Looking at the giant brown markings left by penguins, scientists have estimated that there are more emperor penguin colonies than previously thought.

The Moon

The Moon is Earth's only natural satellite, and it orbits our planet about once a month. Earth's constant companion in space, it has fascinated humans for our entire existence. The Moon causes tides on Earth, illuminates our night sky by reflecting the Sun's light, and was the first place in space that humans explored.

"Born" from a crash

The Moon was part of Earth until about 4.45 billion years ago. At that time, Earth was a hot, melted ball of rock and metal that was frequently crashed into by asteroids. Scientists believe that an asteroid called Theia crashed into Earth, releasing a huge amount of energy.

Moment of impact

When Theia collided with Earth, the impact caused a lot of material to be thrown up into space. This then spun out into a disk around Earth.

Coming together

Over time, the gravity of the largest clump of material in the disk pulled the rest of the material into it. A young, hot, melted Moon was formed. As time passed, the Moon cooled and solidified.

Moon features

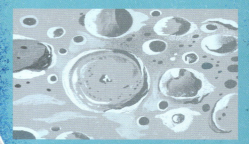

1 Highlands
Highlands are light areas on the surface of the Moon, made of a bright rock called anorthosite. This ancient Moon rock has been repeatedly smashed into by asteroids.

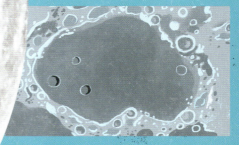

2 Maria
Dark areas are named after the Latin word for "sea" because they look like oceans. They are actually areas of basalt rock, which is common in volcanic areas on Earth.

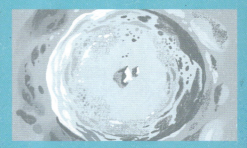

3 Craters
With no atmosphere, the Moon has nothing to protect it from asteroids or comets that collide with it. This means that the Moon's surface is littered with circular impact craters.

The Moon is tidally locked with Earth, which means the same side of it always faces us. Until we sent spacecraft there, we had no idea what the farside of the Moon looked like.

The farside of the Moon

Apollo and Artemis

The Moon has been the target for some amazing space missions, from taking high-resolution pictures from orbit, to sending humans to walk on its surface. Some of our biggest space achievements have been in getting to the Moon, and there is a whole new age of Moon exploration yet to come.

The Space Race

In the 1960s, there was a race between the USA and the former Soviet Union, to see which superpower would be first to send humans to walk on the Moon. It became known as the Space Race. The Soviet Union sent the first human into space, but it was the USA who first placed humans on the Moon. Apollo was the name given to NASA's Moon missions.

Apollo 8

In December 1968, humans left Earth's orbit and travelled to the Moon for the first time. The crew didn't land, but orbited the Moon ten times, testing the technology. They took images of the Moon's surface and of the Earth rising above the Moon before returning safely home.

Apollo 11

"That's one small step for man, one giant leap for mankind." With these words, Neil Armstrong became the first human to set foot on the Moon, in July 1969. For the next 21 hours, he and fellow astronaut Buzz Aldrin would plant the US flag on the surface of the Moon, gather rocks to take back to Earth, and perform experiments.

Apollo 14

In February 1971, NASA astronaut Alan Shepard made a golf club from a piece of equipment. He hit two balls that he had brought with him – a difficult job in a bulky space suit!

Apollo programme highlights

Artemis mission

More than 50 years since humans last set foot on the Moon, NASA decided to return. Its Artemis mission was set up to land the first woman, the first person of colour, and the first non-American on the Moon. The Artemis team planned to do more Moon science than ever before, paving the way for a permanent base on the Moon and testing new technology for future missions to Mars!

New Spacecraft

The Apollo missions could only carry three astronauts to the Moon and two to the surface. The Artemis programme has two new spacecraft, including *Orion*, which can carry four to six astronauts.

Orion →

Naming Artemis

The Apollo programme was named after the Greek god of light, music, and the Sun. Apollo's twin sister is Artemis, so when NASA decided to send the first woman to the Moon, it seemed natural to name the mission after Apollo's sister.

Between December 1968 and December 1972, 12 people walked on the Moon's surface as part of the Apollo Programme.

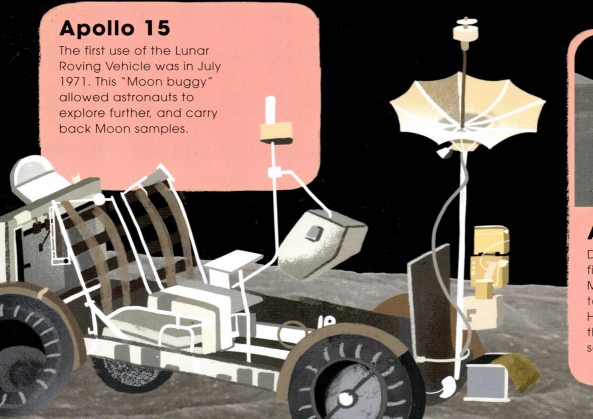

Apollo 15

The first use of the Lunar Roving Vehicle was in July 1971. This "Moon buggy" allowed astronauts to explore further, and carry back Moon samples.

Apollo 17

December 1972 saw Apollo's final crewed mission to the Moon. This was the only mission to carry a scientist, geologist Harrison Schmitt. He chose the most interesting rocks for scientists to study back on Earth.

Robots on the Moon

We haven't sent humans to the Moon for more than 50 years, but that doesn't mean we haven't been studying it. We find out more about the Moon every day, exploring its surface using orbital missions, probes, and Moon rovers and landers.

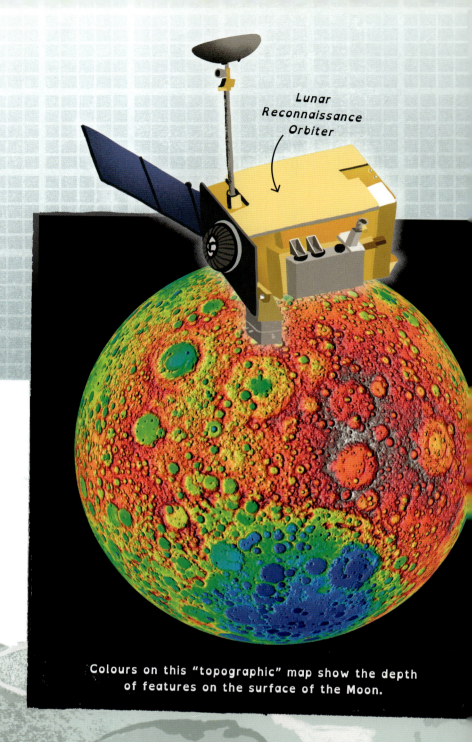

Lunar Reconnaissance Orbiter

Colours on this "topographic" map show the depth of features on the surface of the Moon.

Mapping the Moon

Since 2009, NASA's *Lunar Reconnaissance Orbiter* (*LRO*) has been taking extremely detailed images of the surface of the Moon. Orbiting around the Moon's poles, it has produced 3D maps of the surface that use colour to show the Moon's features in more detail than ever before. These images are vital for planning future Moon missions.

Chandrayaan-1

Hitting the Moon

We don't have humans on the surface collecting rocks, but that doesn't mean we can't get information about what the Moon is made of. In 2008, India's first moon mission launched *Chandrayaan-1*, which sent its *Moon Impact Probe* to hit the surface. The probe discovered that there is frozen water in the lunar soil.

Jade Rabbit

The Chinese Space Agency (CSA) has been making huge strides in Solar System exploration, sending two lunar rovers to the Moon. In December 2013, its Chang'e 3 mission set a lander on the surface, becoming the first controlled landing since 1976. It sent a small rover called *Yutu* (Jade Rabbit) with a special device called a radar, which was used to create images of the area below the surface of the Moon.

Naming spacecraft

Space exploration has a history of naming missions and spacecraft to reflect culture and history. In the case of China's Moon missions, the Chang'e landers are named after the Chinese goddess of the Moon, and the *Yutu* rovers after the "Jade Rabbit", which lives on the Moon according to Chinese folklore. If you look at the Moon, you might see where this myth came from.

Landing on the farside

On 3 January 2019, China's Chang'e 4 became the first mission ever to land successfully on the farside of the Moon. This mission was especially difficult because you can't directly communicate with a spacecraft on the farside of the Moon – the Moon gets in the way!

The CSA put a communications satellite in orbit, to allow engineers to talk to the rover on the farside of the Moon.

Chang'e 4 Lander

Mars

Mars is the fourth planet from the Sun and the last of the terrestrial (rocky) planets. It is about half the size of Earth. Mars is known as the Red Planet due to its colour, which it gets from iron oxide (rust) in its soil. With a thin atmosphere of mainly carbon dioxide gas, Mars is a barren world. Evidence on the surface of Mars suggests that it was once much more Earth-like than it is today.

Freezing desert

Mars is very cold. Its average temperature is around −65°C (−85°F). Mars also has an incredibly thin atmosphere, which is less than 1 per cent as thick as Earth's. This means that liquid water cannot exist for long on the surface of Mars, making it a cold, desert planet. The thin atmosphere also means that meteorites have regularly slammed into Mars, scarring it with craters.

The scar across the surface of Mars is Valles Marineris, a canyon that's 4,000 km (2,500 miles) long.

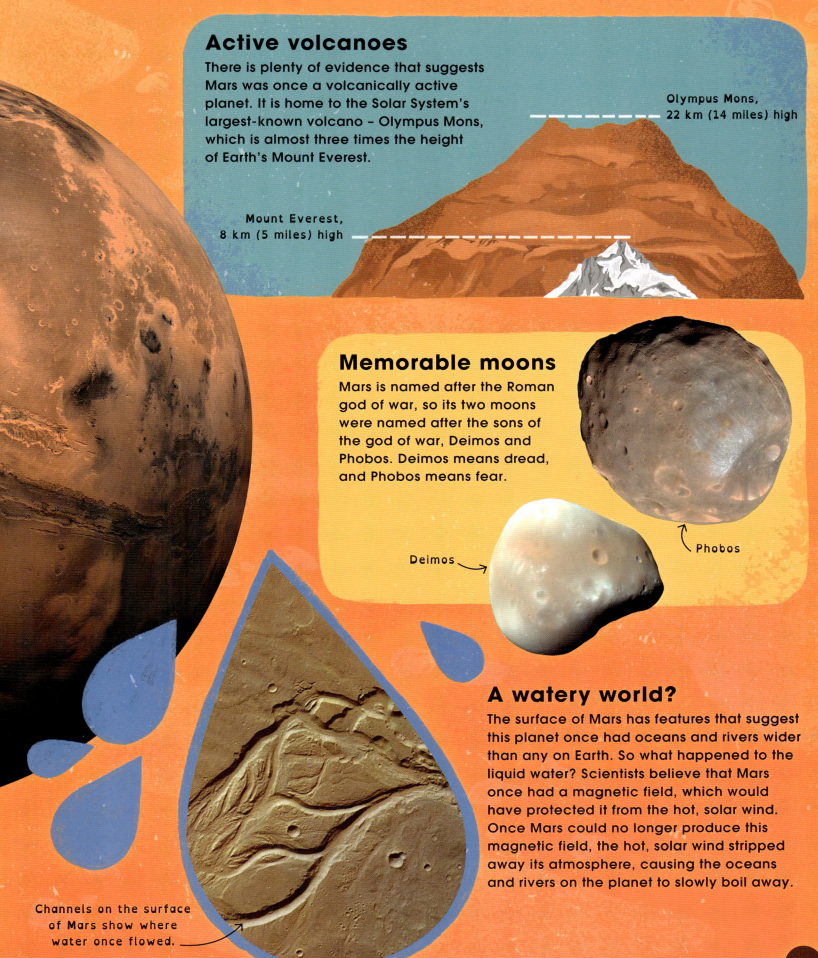

Active volcanoes

There is plenty of evidence that suggests Mars was once a volcanically active planet. It is home to the Solar System's largest-known volcano – Olympus Mons, which is almost three times the height of Earth's Mount Everest.

Olympus Mons, 22 km (14 miles) high

Mount Everest, 8 km (5 miles) high

Memorable moons

Mars is named after the Roman god of war, so its two moons were named after the sons of the god of war, Deimos and Phobos. Deimos means dread, and Phobos means fear.

Phobos

Deimos

A watery world?

The surface of Mars has features that suggest this planet once had oceans and rivers wider than any on Earth. So what happened to the liquid water? Scientists believe that Mars once had a magnetic field, which would have protected it from the hot, solar wind. Once Mars could no longer produce this magnetic field, the hot, solar wind stripped away its atmosphere, causing the oceans and rivers on the planet to slowly boil away.

Channels on the surface of Mars show where water once flowed.

Exploring Mars

Of all the planets in the Solar System, Mars has been explored the most. However, exploring Mars is challenging, and around half of all missions to the planet have ended in failure. As our technology improves, so does our ability to explore and understand the Red Planet. From satellites in orbit taking photos and scanning the surface, to rover adventurers performing experiments, space scientists are always learning more about Mars.

Rovers are remote-controlled vehicles. Here, their tyre tracks can be seen in the dust on the surface of Mars.

Opportunity

Spirit

Spirit and Opportunity

In 2004, NASA landed twin rovers, *Spirit* and *Opportunity*, on separate parts of Mars. The two solar-powered rovers carried out work to help prove that Mars was once hotter and wetter than it is now, and that it had the environment needed to support simple life, called microbes. Both rovers worked for much longer than their planned 90 days. *Opportunity* worked for nearly 15 years!

Mars has hills and valleys that look similar to Earth's.

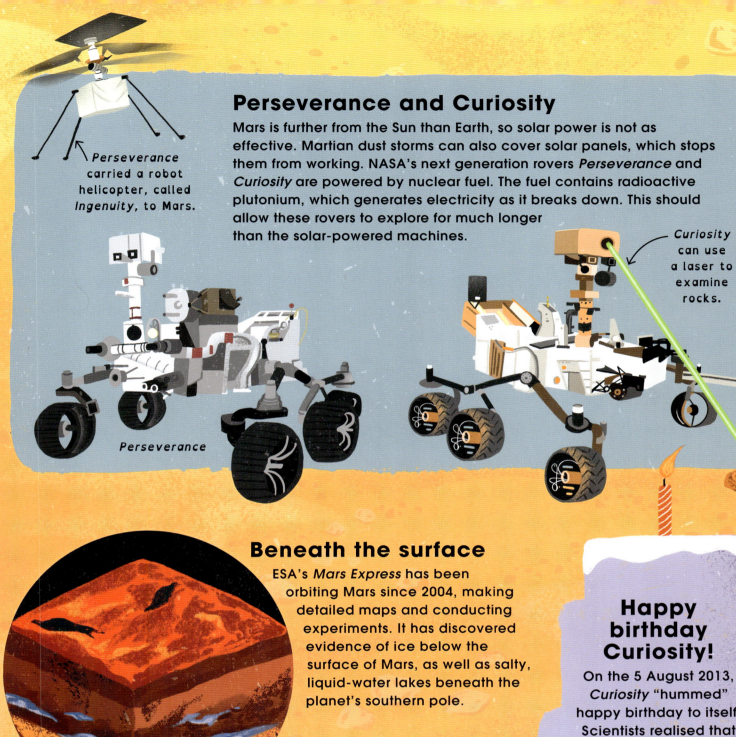

Perseverance and Curiosity

Mars is further from the Sun than Earth, so solar power is not as effective. Martian dust storms can also cover solar panels, which stops them from working. NASA's next generation rovers *Perseverance* and *Curiosity* are powered by nuclear fuel. The fuel contains radioactive plutonium, which generates electricity as it breaks down. This should allow these rovers to explore for much longer than the solar-powered machines.

Perseverance carried a robot helicopter, called Ingenuity, to Mars.

Perseverance

Curiosity can use a laser to examine rocks.

Beneath the surface

ESA's *Mars Express* has been orbiting Mars since 2004, making detailed maps and conducting experiments. It has discovered evidence of ice below the surface of Mars, as well as salty, liquid-water lakes beneath the planet's southern pole.

Happy birthday Curiosity!

On the 5 August 2013, *Curiosity* "hummed" happy birthday to itself! Scientists realised that they could control one of *Curiosity's* scientific instruments to make the humming noise. This lonely celebration was the first-ever performance by a human-built object on Mars.

CHAPTER 3

THE BELT
AND BEYOND

Between Mars and Jupiter is a band of rocky objects
called the Asteroid Belt. The planets beyond the Belt
are vastly different to our own.

Four planets orbit the Sun after the Asteroid Belt: Jupiter, Saturn, Uranus,
and Neptune. They are giant planets, with many moons. These moons offer us
the best chances of finding life beyond Earth. At the very edge of the Solar System
are cold, frozen worlds that remain relatively unexplored. These mysterious worlds
may hold many more space secrets that are just waiting to be discovered...

Between Mars and the gas giants lies the Asteroid Belt.
This area of space contains millions of asteroids – chunks
of rock and metal that orbit the Sun. Some are as small as
a car, others as big as a moon. The Belt contains some of
the oldest material in our Solar System, including asteroids
that have remained largely unchanged for 4.5 billion years!

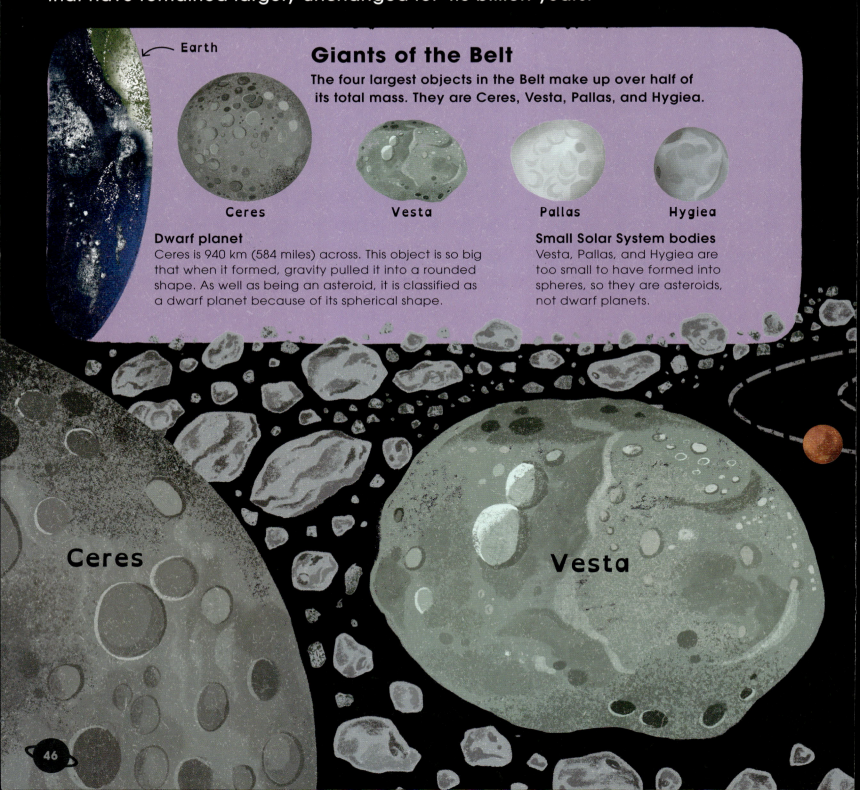

Earth

Giants of the Belt

The four largest objects in the Belt make up over half of
its total mass. They are Ceres, Vesta, Pallas, and Hygiea.

Ceres

Vesta

Pallas

Hygiea

Dwarf planet
Ceres is 940 km (584 miles) across. This object is so big
that when it formed, gravity pulled it into a rounded
shape. As well as being an asteroid, it is classified as
a dwarf planet because of its spherical shape.

Small Solar System bodies
Vesta, Pallas, and Hygiea are
too small to have formed into
spheres, so they are asteroids,
not dwarf planets.

Ceres

Vesta

Crossing the Belt

You might think that a spacecraft travelling through the Asteroid Belt would get hit, but this isn't a worry for space scientists. There is actually a lot of space between asteroids. In fact, if you sent a billion spacecraft through the Belt, only one would get hit! Twelve spacecraft have journeyed safely through the Belt so far.

In 1973, *Pioneer 10* became the first spacecraft to pass through the Asteroid Belt, on its way to Jupiter.

All in a name

Space rocks are named depending on where they are in relation to Earth.

Meteoroid
This is a relatively small piece of an asteroid that hasn't entered Earth's atmosphere. It can also be a piece of a comet (a huge lump of rocky ice) that hasn't entered Earth's atmosphere.

Meteor
This is a meteoroid that has entered Earth's atmosphere. The space rock gets very hot and starts to "burn up", becoming a bright streak of light in the sky.

Meteorite
If a meteor makes it to Earth's surface, what survives the impact is known as a meteorite.

Put together, all the material in the Asteroid Belt is smaller than Earth's Moon.

Precious materials

Asteroids often contain useful metals, such as iron and nickel, but some also contain precious metals, such as gold and platinum. For years, people have dreamed of mining asteroids to extract their raw materials, using robotic spacecraft or even humans. For now, the cost is too high, and asteroid mining is a long way off.

Jupiter

The fifth planet from the Sun is huge. Earth could fit into Jupiter more than 1,000 times. Jupiter also has more than twice the mass (amount of matter) of all the other planets added together. A gas giant without a solid surface, Jupiter is made mostly of hydrogen and helium. It spins very fast – a day on Jupiter is less than 10 hours long.

What's inside?

At the centre of Jupiter is a solid core of ice, rock, and metal. A layer of squashed hydrogen above the core acts like liquid metal, and a layer of cold, liquid hydrogen sits above that. The surface layer is mainly hydrogen and helium gas, with beautiful ammonia clouds.

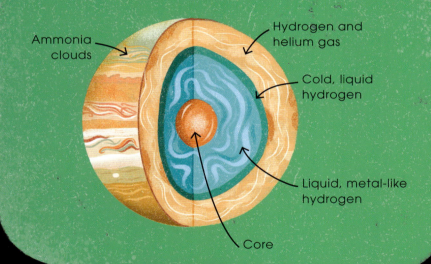

Ammonia clouds

Hydrogen and helium gas

Cold, liquid hydrogen

Liquid, metal-like hydrogen

Core

Visits to Jupiter

Many space missions have flown by Jupiter, but few have focused on just this planet. The first spacecraft to orbit Jupiter was called *Galileo*.

Galileo carried a small probe, which investigated Jupiter's atmosphere.

Spectacular storms

As Jupiter is so enormous, and spins so fast, its atmosphere gets whipped up into beautiful bands. There is so much energy here that huge storms form, which can rage for years.

Jupiter's Great Red Spot is a giant hurricane that has been going on for hundreds of years.

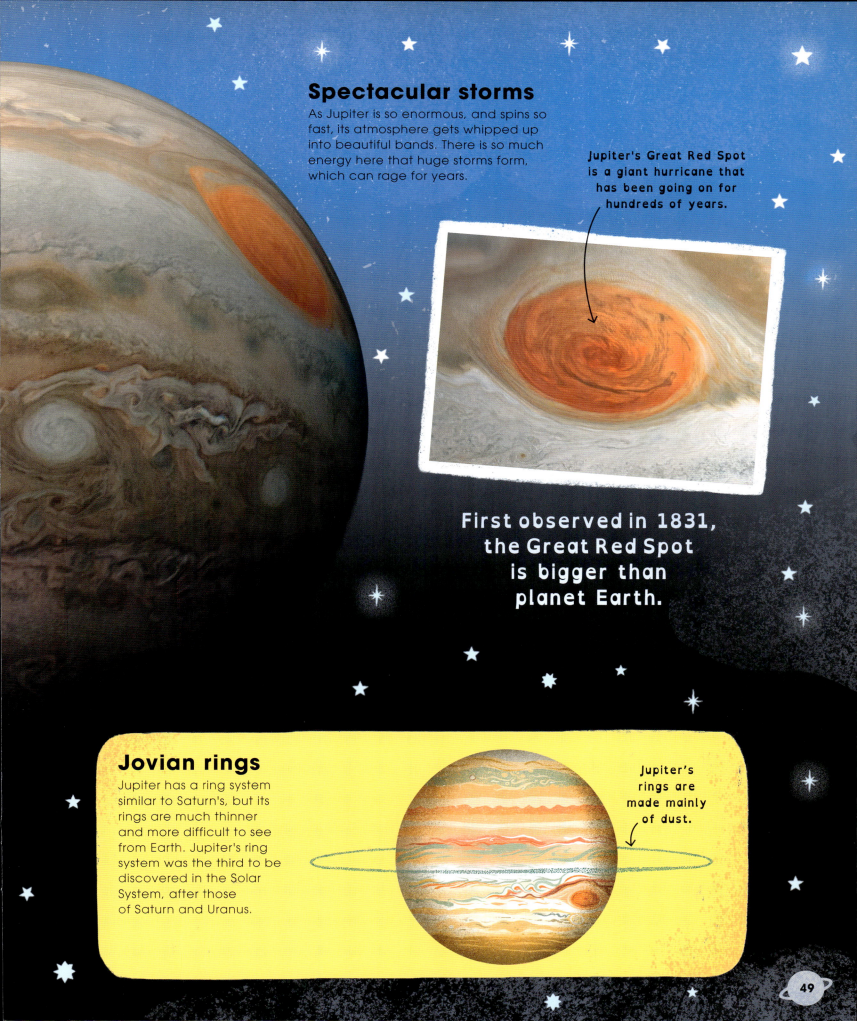

First observed in 1831, the Great Red Spot is bigger than planet Earth.

Jovian rings

Jupiter has a ring system similar to Saturn's, but its rings are much thinner and more difficult to see from Earth. Jupiter's ring system was the third to be discovered in the Solar System, after those of Saturn and Uranus.

Jupiter's rings are made mainly of dust.

Jupiter's moons

Jupiter holds the title of biggest planet in the Solar System, and takes second place in the competition for planet with the most moons. Jupiter's four largest moons – Io, Callisto, Ganymede, and Europa – are known as the Galilean moons. They were the first moons to be discovered orbiting another planet.

Io

The closest moon to Jupiter, Io is caught in a gravity tug of war between Jupiter and the other Galilean moons. This constant pushing and pulling heats the moon up, melting the inside. This has made Io the most volcanic place in our Solar System – it constantly spurts its heated insides out above its surface!

Io's surface is made of sulphur.

Callisto's bright spots are craters.

Callisto

Callisto is a heavily-cratered ice world. It is extensively scarred with ancient impact craters that were made by comets and meteors. Some craters are thought to be around 4 billion years old! Scientists used to think that there could be an ocean below the surface of Callisto, but recent research suggests that it is either deeper than they thought, or that it may not exist at all.

Some of Callisto's craters are believed to be the oldest in the Solar System.

Jupiter has more than 92 moons, so scientists have decided to give grand names only to those that are of particular interest or importance.

Light areas are grooves and ice-tipped ridges.

Ganymede

The largest moon in the Solar System, Ganymede is bigger than the planet Mercury. It is made of rock and ice and has a cold, icy surface. Scientists believe there may be a huge, saltwater ocean trapped below the ice.

Dark areas are old craters.

Flat, icy surface, which looks like an ocean covered in cracked ice.

Europa

Europa is an ice moon that has excited scientists for years. It is of particular interest to astrobiologists who are searching for life elsewhere in our Solar System. Europa is thought to have a huge, liquid ocean beneath a relatively thin, icy surface. The bottom of Europa's ocean may have hydrothermal vents – openings in the ocean floor that eject hot, mineral-rich water – like those on Earth. If this is the case, then small forms of life that are adapted to survive in extreme environments could live there.

Europa is the smallest of the Galilean moons.

Saturn's stormy crown

Saturn has a complex weather system and a jet stream – a narrow stream of extremely strong wind that impacts the weather. This jet stream is a hexagon shape and it causes the gases at the planet's northern pole to be whipped up into a hexagonal storm that is 30,000 km (18,641 miles) wide – roughly twice the width of planet Earth!

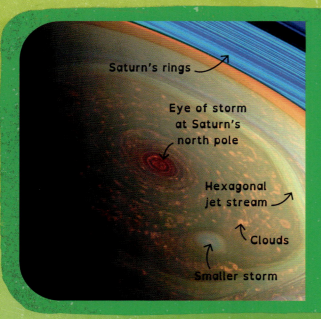

Saturn's rings

Eye of storm at Saturn's north pole

Hexagonal jet stream

Clouds

Smaller storm

A ring

B ring

C ring

D ring

Saturn's main rings have been assigned the letters of the alphabet as their names, in the order they were discovered.

The *Cassini* spacecraft explored Saturn. It orbited the planet between 2004 and 2017.

Cassini's first image of Saturn.

Saturn

Saturn is the sixth planet from the Sun, and is most famous for its spectacular rings. Like Jupiter, it is a gas giant – a huge ball of mostly hydrogen and helium gas. Saturn has a short day of approximately 10.7 hours, and a long year equal to 29.4 Earth years.

Icy rings

Saturn's rings are formed from a mixture of things, from tiny fragments of ice to giant boulders that can be as big as a mountain. Scientists believe that the rings formed when comets and asteroids broke up before reaching the planet. The pieces were then sucked into orbit by Saturn's gravity.

Ice in Saturn's rings reflects light. That's why we see the rings so well.

"Yearly" storms

Saturn has enormous storms, known as Great White Spots, that happen around every 30 Earth years. While that may seem like a long time, Saturn's year is just less than 30 Earth years, so it is a yearly event on Saturn. Over time, each of these Great White Spots can develop a long tail that encircles the planet. In late 2010 and early 2011, the *Cassini* spacecraft was perfectly placed to capture images of a Great White Spot.

Great White Spot with tail circling Saturn

Image captured by *Cassini*

Shepherd moons

Many of Saturn's moons are positioned in between its rings. Their presence shapes the planet's ring structure, because their gravity "herds" any stray particles of ice and dust into Saturn's rings.

The gaps between Saturn's rings are areas with fewer pieces of ice and dust.

Saturn's moons

Saturn is thought to have more than 145 moons – more than any other planet. However, it's not just the large number of moons that is interesting. Scientists are excited by the moons' features, too – they seem to include strange, alien worlds, and frozen landscapes.

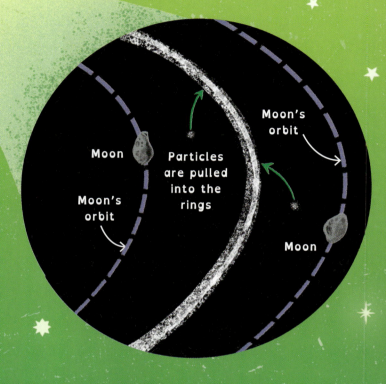

Moon

Moon's orbit

Particles are pulled into the rings

Moon's orbit

Moon

Titan is the most Earth-like place in the Solar System.

Titan

Titan is the second biggest moon in the Solar System – it is bigger than the planet Mercury. Titan is the only moon that has a thick atmosphere, which can make it challenging to observe. However, scientists have discovered rivers, lakes, and seas of liquid methane on Titan's surface. Observations have also shown that there is weather on Titan.

Enceladus

Most planets and moons are scarred by meteorite impacts. Enceladus is an ice moon with a smooth surface, which suggests that something has been "repairing" it after impacts. The *Cassini* spacecraft flew through an eruption of liquid water, called a geyser, from Enceladus. This led to the discovery of a liquid ocean below the moon's surface.

Enceladus is the whitest object in our Solar System.

Geysers spurt liquid water from Enceladus.

Mimas

The smallest of Saturn's major moons, Mimas takes just under one Earth day to orbit the planet. It is a ball of ice measuring 400 km (248 miles) across, with a surface covered with impact craters. The biggest of these is the Herschel crater, which is 80 km (50 miles) across.

The Herschel crater is named after astronomer William Herschel.

The moons to scale

Saturn's moons come in a huge range of sizes. Titan is considerably bigger than any of the other moons, many of which are no bigger than a football stadium.

Mimas

Enceladus

Titan

Saturn

Studying Saturn

Much of what we know about Saturn is a result of the hugely ambitious Cassini-Huygens mission. This NASA-ESA collaboration achieved several groundbreaking space firsts, and took breathtaking images of Saturn. The mission ended with a memorable event that left its mark on the planet – forever.

Mission firsts

Cassini-Huygens was a trailblazing mission.

 It was the first mission ever to orbit Saturn

 First to sample water from an alien ocean

 First to land on an object beyond the Asteroid Belt

 First to be purposefully crashed into Saturn

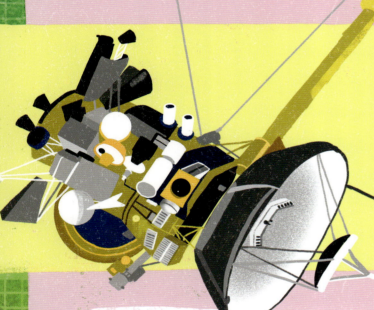

Cassini

In October 1997, NASA's *Cassini* spacecraft began a 7-year journey to Saturn. Entering orbit around Saturn in 2004, it travelled around the planet for 13 years. *Cassini* investigated Saturn and photographed its rings, moons, and surface, producing images that were better than any before.

Saturn's rings

Cassini imaged Saturn's iconic rings with the Sun behind and above them, for the first time in history. Scientists used the shadows cast by objects in the rings to estimate their size, showing that they are actually razor-thin!

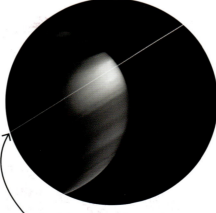

A side view shows how thin Saturn's rings are.

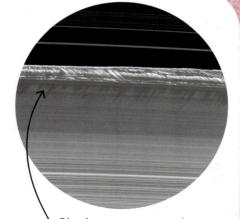

Shadows were used to measure the rings.

Space passenger

Cassini carried an important passenger on its journey: ESA's *Huygens* spacecraft. Scientists had long speculated about the possibility of lakes on one of Saturn's moons, Titan. *Huygens* used radar to allow scientists to "see" through Titan's thick atmosphere and observe exactly what lay on its surface.

Exploring Titan

Huygens captured stunning images as it descended through the haze of Titan's atmosphere. There were mountains made of ice, and an icy surface covered with chemicals. Rivers and lakes of liquid methane, clouds, and weather patterns could also be seen. It didn't look too different from Earth.

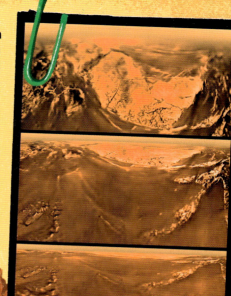

Images were taken at different heights as the probe moved closer.

A careful landing

In 2007, *Huygens* was released towards the surface of Titan. Parachutes slowed the spacecraft, allowing it to carefully land. The descent took a nail-biting 2.5 hours, but it worked! This was the first time anything ever landed on an object located beyond the Asteroid Belt.

Huygens was designed to float if it landed on a liquid.

Mission complete

After 20 years of service, *Cassini* was running out of fuel. On 15 September 2017 it was sent on a carefully planned dive towards the centre of Saturn, to make sure a collision didn't damage the planet's ring structure.

Cassini's legacy

- 20 years of service
- 7.9 billion km (4.9 billion miles) travelled
- 294 orbits of Saturn
- 162 targeted flybys of Saturn's moons
- 453,048 images captured

Uranus

This is the seventh planet from the Sun, and the third-largest in the Solar System. Uranus is an ice giant. Like the gas giants Jupiter and Saturn, Uranus has an atmosphere of mainly hydrogen and helium gas. But below that lies a frozen layer of water, ammonia, and methane. Uranus has 27 moons, and a faint ring system.

Gas giant or ice giant?

Jupiter and Saturn are gas giants, while Uranus and Neptune are ice giants. So, what is the difference between them?

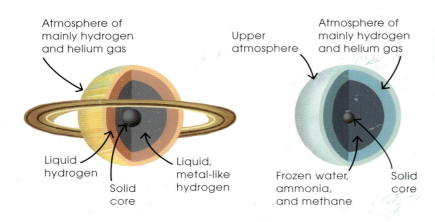

Atmosphere of mainly hydrogen and helium gas

Upper atmosphere

Atmosphere of mainly hydrogen and helium gas

Liquid hydrogen

Solid core

Liquid, metal-like hydrogen

Frozen water, ammonia, and methane

Solid core

Gas giants
Gas giants have small, dense, rocky cores surrounded by a completely gaseous structure. They have a thick atmosphere of mainly hydrogen and helium.

Ice giants
Ice giants also have a dense, rocky core, but smaller than the cores of the gas giants. They are colder than the gas giants, and have a layer of frozen water, ammonia, and methane around the core.

Uranus was the first planet to be discovered using a telescope, by Astronomer William Herschel, in 1781.

As well as hydrogen and helium, there is
a little methane in Uranus' atmosphere.
The methane absorbs red light from the Sun,
creating the blue-green colour of Uranus.

Uranus' rings appear
to loop around it
vertically because
it spins on its side.

A planet of extremes

Uranus is a strange planet in many ways. Like
Venus, it rotates in the opposite direction to the
other planets – from east to west instead of west
to east. Uranus is tilted on its side by 98°, which
means it also rotates in a different plane to the other
planets. Scientists think its tilt was probably the result
of a collision when it was a young planet. This huge
tilt gives Uranus the most extreme seasons of any
planet in our Solar System. Winter on Uranus is 21 years
long, without any sunlight.

Uranus spins on
its side. This arrow
shows how it spins.

Mercury
0° tilt

Earth
23° tilt

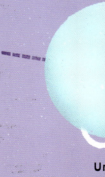

Uranus
98° tilt

Neptune

Neptune is the eighth planet in the Solar System, and the furthest from the Sun. Like Uranus, Neptune is an ice giant. It has the longest year of all the planets, taking 165 Earth years to orbit the Sun. Neptune has a small, faint ring system and only 14 known moons, fewer than the other giant planets. It is so far away from Earth that it cannot be seen with the naked eye.

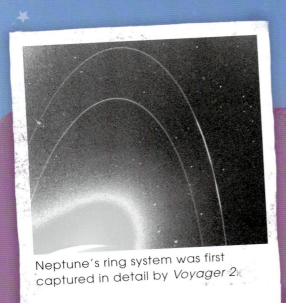

Neptune's ring system was first captured in detail by *Voyager 2*.

The lonely planet

Neptune has only been briefly visited by one spacecraft. In 1989, *Voyager 2* took images of this ice giant as it flew past on its way out of the Solar System. No spacecraft has ever orbited Neptune.

 Voyager 2

Finding Neptune

After Uranus was discovered in 1781, astronomers noticed that its orbit would speed up or slow down at different times. This made them think that there must be another large planet that they couldn't see, and that its gravity was affecting Uranus. Using observations and mathematical calculations, they attempted to predict this planet's location. In September 1846, an astronomer called Johann Galle turned his telescope to the predicted location and discovered the eighth planet of the Solar System – Neptune.

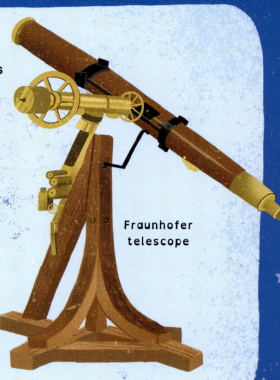

Fraunhofer telescope

Johann Galle used a wooden telescope developed by Joseph von Fraunhofer to search for the new planet.

Mysterious moon

Neptune's biggest moon is called Triton. It is the only major moon in our Solar System that moves around its planet in the opposite direction to that planet's rotation. This is called a "retrograde orbit". Triton also spins on its axis in the opposite direction to Neptune. Scientists think Triton probably formed separately from Neptune, but became captured by Neptune's gravity.

Triton is the biggest of Neptune's known moons, and the seventh-largest moon in the Solar System.

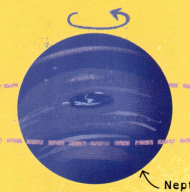

Triton

Triton's orbit

Neptune

The problem with Pluto

Pluto orbits the Sun beyond Neptune, in the Kuiper Belt. It was first discovered by an American astronomer, Clyde Tombaugh, in 1930. For years Pluto was thought of as a planet, equal to Mercury, Venus, Earth, Mars, Jupiter, Saturn, Uranus, and Neptune. In 2006 this changed, and Pluto became known as a dwarf planet rather than a full planet. But why?

Planet checklist

What does it take to be a true planet? If you can tick all the boxes below, congratulations, you are a planet!

- ✓ Orbits the Sun

- ✓ Has enough mass to be spherical (round)

- ✗ Is big enough that it has swept its orbit clear of other objects

A dwarf planet

Pluto doesn't meet the conditions needed to be named a true planet – it is too small to have swept its orbit clear of other material. Pluto was reclassified as a dwarf planet because of its small size and inability to pull all local material into it's orbit. Don't feel too bad for Pluto though – it has five moons and plenty of company in its part of space, which is called the Kuiper Belt.

The Kuiper Belt is a band of objects that orbits the Sun, beyond the orbit of Neptune.

Kuiper Belt

Pluto's orbit

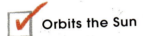

The Sun

Pluto

In 2006, Pluto was recognized as a dwarf planet, and the largest object to move through the Kuiper Belt.

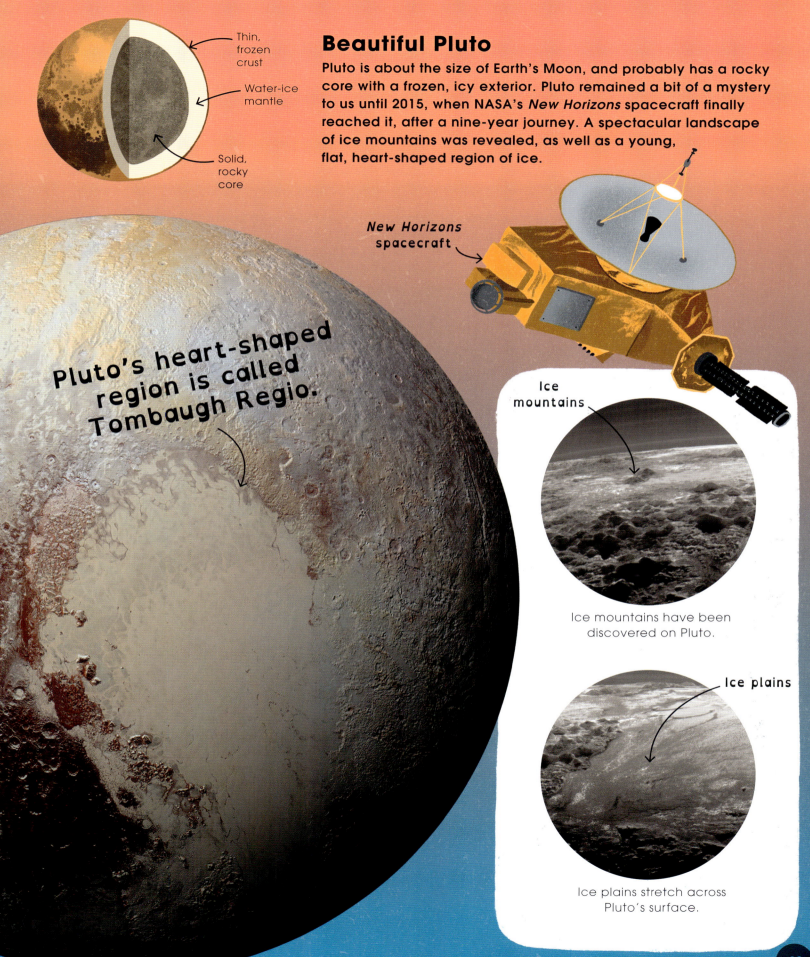

Thin, frozen crust

Water-ice mantle

Solid, rocky core

Beautiful Pluto

Pluto is about the size of Earth's Moon, and probably has a rocky core with a frozen, icy exterior. Pluto remained a bit of a mystery to us until 2015, when NASA's *New Horizons* spacecraft finally reached it, after a nine-year journey. A spectacular landscape of ice mountains was revealed, as well as a young, flat, heart-shaped region of ice.

New Horizons spacecraft

Pluto's heart-shaped region is called Tombaugh Regio.

Ice mountains

Ice mountains have been discovered on Pluto.

Ice plains

Ice plains stretch across Pluto's surface.

Beyond the planets

Far, far beyond the planets exists a freezing, dark sphere of icy objects called the Oort Cloud. The Oort Cloud is so far away that scientists have never directly seen it. They have predicted that it must be there by tracking the orbits of comets that have travelled close to the Sun. The Oort Cloud is thought to be home to hundreds of billions of comets.

The Oort Cloud

The Solar System

Comets

Comets are large objects made of dust and ice – materials left over from when the Solar System formed. Comets exist in the Kuiper Belt and the Oort Cloud, and can be knocked into a special type of squashed orbit around the Sun, called an elliptical orbit.

Comet

As a comet gets close to the Sun, it begins to warm up. Its ice turns into a gas, and dust is released. This creates a cloud, called a coma, with a solid part at the centre, called the nucleus.

Two tails form as dust and gas flow away from a comet. The tails point away from the Sun, pushed by the solar wind as the comet orbits.

Comet's orbit

The Sun and solar wind

Dust tail   Gases

The Oort Cloud is 50,000 times further away from the Sun than the Earth is!

A spectacular show!

When comets get very close to the Sun, we can see them in the night sky for a week or more.

Sometimes, the Earth passes through the dust tails left behind by a comet. When this happens, dust and material from the comet burn up in the atmosphere, producing spectacular streaks of light, called meteor showers.

Rosetta and Philae

In 2014, ESA's *Rosetta* spacecraft reached Comet 67P/Churyumov-Gerasimenko after a 10-year journey. The *Rosetta* had an ambitious mission – to release a probe called *Philae* to study the comet. But *Philae's* anchoring harpoons didn't work. Instead of landing, the probe bounced! It landed in the shadow of a cliff, limiting its solar power. After two days it ran out of energy – but not before making history as the first mission to land on a comet.

Rosetta

Philae

Streams of gas escape as Comet 67-P heats up. The comet appears to be the result of a collision between two smaller comets.

CHAPTER 4

OUR SOLAR SYSTEM AND US

Scientists constantly develop new technology and scientific methods, which help us understand our Solar System better.

Studying our Solar System teaches us about our neighbourhood as it is now, and studying other stars and planets helps us to predict how it will be in billions of years. New, innovative ways of looking at space allow us to see it in ever-clearer detail. Read on to learn more about what the future holds for our Solar System, and what space scientists are planning to do next.

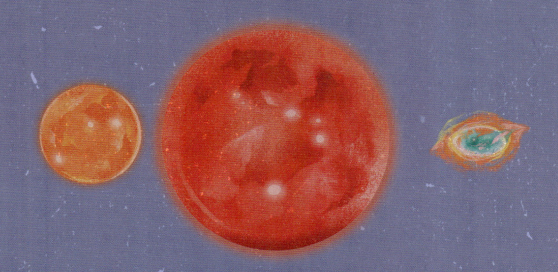

Our Solar System's fate

The life of our Solar System is entirely linked to the life of our star, the Sun. The planets are held in orbit around the Sun by its gravity, and the temperature and seasons of the planets all depend on heat and light from the Sun. The future of our entire Solar System is linked to the future of the Sun.

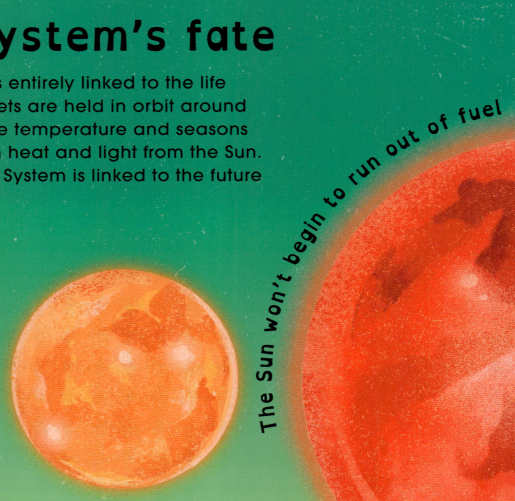

The Sun won't begin to run out of fuel

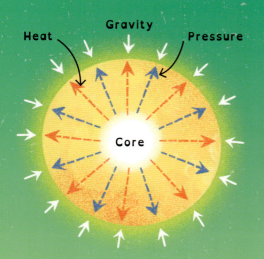

Heat
Gravity
Pressure

Core

Balancing the Sun

Inside our fiery Sun is a constant battle between gravity making the gases of the Sun collapse in, and pressure from the nuclear fusion inside the Sun making it expand outwards. For now, the forces are balanced.

Our Sun today
The Sun is a giant, nuclear machine, smashing hydrogen together to form helium and produce energy (fusion), which keeps it burning bright. But what will happen when it runs out of fuel?

Timeline of the Sun

Birth of the Sun | 1 billion years | 2 | 3 | 4 | 5 | 6 | 7 | 8 | 9

Sun's current age

As it runs out of fuel, the Sun will start to collapse, which will make it heat up again.

for at least 5 billion years!

Gobbling up the inner planets

In billions of years, when the Sun becomes a red giant, it will expand and gobble up Mercury, Venus, and possibly Earth. Mars will become extremely hot. Jupiter and Saturn will be in the habitable zone – the region of space around the Sun that is where liquid water can exist.

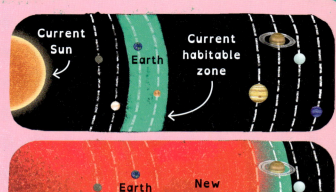

Current Sun
Earth
Current habitable zone

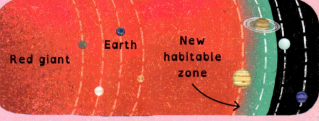

Red giant
Earth
New habitable zone

Running out of fuel

As the Sun begins to run out of fuel to burn, it will collapse inwards, which will cause it to get really hot again. It will then expand, get bigger and cooler, and become a red giant star.

A spectacular show

Eventually, the Sun will run completely out of fuel. It will collapse in on itself, releasing its outer layers into space. A spectacular collection of gas called a planetary nebula will be created.

Getting colder

Finally, all that will remain of the Sun will be its core – a small, hot star known as a white dwarf. Over time, the white dwarf will get cooler and fainter until the Solar System goes dark.

The future...

Humans have only been around for a tiny part of the Solar System's existence. In fact, if you think of our Solar System as being born 24 hours ago, then humans have only been around for a few seconds! We have plenty of time left to explore space. Perhaps one day, humans will even venture beyond our Solar System!

10   11   12   13   14

Red giant

Planetary nebula

White dwarf – typically around the same size as Earth.

The James Webb Space Telescope

Launched on 25 December 2021, the James Webb Space Telescope is the biggest telescope ever sent into space. It is helping us redefine our understanding of the Solar System by taking extraordinary images, which are different to anything we have seen before. These pictures allow scientists to investigate what atmospheres and nebulae (giant clouds of dust and gas in space) are made of.

Space origami

The Webb Telescope uses infrared light, which has a longer wavelength than visible light. This allows it to look far out into space and back into our Solar System. It also has a huge sunshield made of several layers of material, which reflects the Sun's heat away from the telescope. Too big to launch on any existing rockets, the telescope had to be folded for its launch, and then unfolded on the way to its destination.

Unfolded sunshield

Sunshield unfolds

Folded telescope

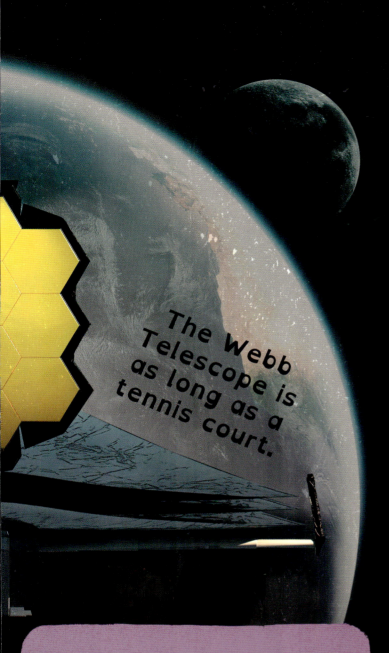

The Webb Telescope is as long as a tennis court.

New views of our Solar System

The Webb Telescope has already made some amazing discoveries within our Solar System. Here are just a few of them:

Jupiter is glowing!

Jupiter experiences aurora – northern and southern lights, just like Earth. The Webb Telescope has shown us just how incredible these lights are. It has also shown us the giant planet's thin ring system clearly for the first time.

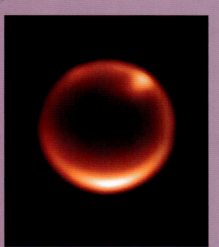

Weather on Titan

Saturn's giant moon, Titan, is the only moon in the Solar System with a thick atmosphere. The Webb Telescope has found cloud systems inside this atmosphere, proving that Titan also has weather.

Galatea · Despina · Naiad · Larissa · Thalassa

Neptune's rings and moons

The Webb Telescope has captured stunning images of Neptune's rings, and some of its moons.

Too far to fix

The Webb telescope is a long way from the Earth. It orbits at a special point in space called a "Lagrange point", or L2. This gives it a clear view into space, while also allowing the Earth to block some of the infrared from the Sun, which would interfere with the telescope. However, it is too far away for humans to be able to fix it, so everything had to unfold perfectly – and it did!

James Webb
Space Telescope

Earth · Moon

Webb is 1.5 million km (1 million miles) away from the Earth, and orbits the Sun.

Views from the Webb Space Telescope

The James Webb telescope is not only giving us new views of our Solar System, but of the whole Universe. It is looking at the oldest, most distant galaxies to help us understand how our Universe formed and where it is going. It is even searching for exoplanets – alien worlds that orbit stars other than the Sun.

Image taken by the Webb telescope in 2022.

Image of the "Pillars of Creation" taken by the Hubble telescope in 1995.

Distant galaxies

The Webb telescope is a big upgrade on previous space telescopes, and can see in greater detail than ever before. By using different types of infrared light, it can look at different things, including gas, planets, and the structure of gas clouds in space.

Finding solar systems

The Webb telescope is hunting for exoplanets. We have already discovered more than 5,000 exoplanets in nearly 4,000 solar systems. Webb will see them more clearly, analyze their atmospheres, and search for new ones.

Hunting for exoplanets

Exoplanets are so small and far away that they are hard to see directly. One of the ways the Webb telescope is looking for them is by viewing the light from stars. When an exoplanet passes in front of a distant star during its orbit, it blocks some of the light from the star, making it look dimmer. The Webb telescope can detect this dimming.

This diagram shows what happens to a star's light when an exoplanet passes in front of it.

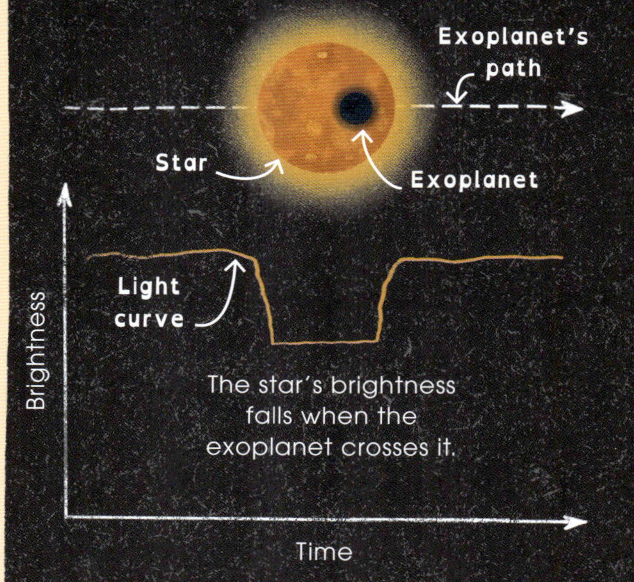

Exoplanet's path

Star

Exoplanet

Brightness

Light curve

The star's brightness falls when the exoplanet crosses it.

Time

The Webb space telescope allows us to learn more about objects we have already studied, including the "Pillars of Creation" in this image.

Solar System selfies

If you were exploring one of the planets, moons, or comets in our Solar System, you'd probably snap a selfie! Robotic spacecraft are no different. All rover missions carry cameras, taking images for scientists to analyze so that engineers can check on the health of the spacecraft. So Solar System selfies have become a trend!

Stitched-together selfie

Taking a space selfie isn't always easy! The *Curiosity* rover took this selfie using the WATSON camera, which is mounted on a robotic arm. However, the camera is designed to take close-up pictures of rocks, not a zoomed-out selfie. So to create this image, the robotic arm moved position while the camera took 62 shots of the rover. These were then stitched together to make a full image.

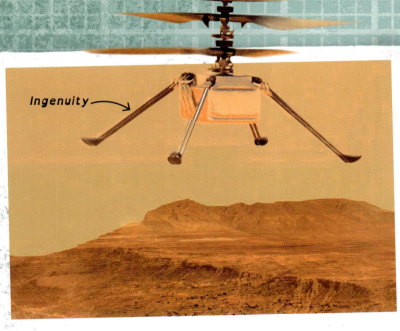

Ingenuity

Action shot!

Sometimes you need a friend to take an amazing action shot of you. Flying on Mars is an incredible achievement, and the *Perseverance* rover was there to snap the *Ingenuity* helicopter in action. This image of *Ingenuity*'s second flight was captured by one of the cameras on *Perseverance*'s mast.

The first spacecraft ever to take a selfie was called Viking 2. The image was taken on Mars in 1976.

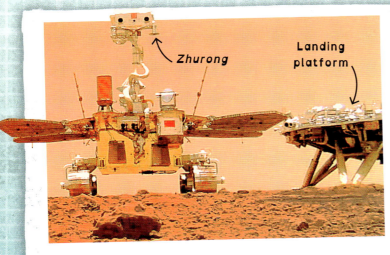

Zhurong

Landing platform

Holiday snaps

China's first rover mission to Mars has taken Solar System selfies to a new level. The *Zhurong* rover carried a specialized, remote camera to the planet. It placed the camera on the ground to get this amazing shot of itself next to the landing platform that delivered it safely to the planet's surface.

The first human space selfie was taken by astronaut Buzz Aldrin, during a Gemini 12 mission in 1966.

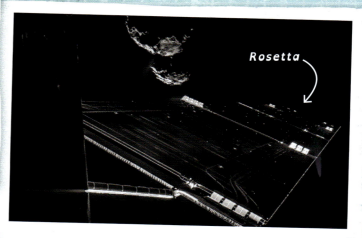

Rosetta

The space influencer

If spacecraft had social media accounts, then *Rosetta's* would probably have the best selfie gallery. Not only did it get an amazing selfie with a comet, but it also took a quick selfie with Mars in the background as it flew by!

First selfie from December 2018

Life on film

Spacecraft selfies help engineers keep track of how the equipment is faring, all alone in space. These are the first and last selfies taken by the *INSIGHT* lander, a mission to study Marsquakes. You can see that a huge amount of dust has built up on the solar panels during the four years between these selfies. In fact, there was so much dust that *INSIGHT* was no longer able to generate enough solar power to function, and was no longer able to communicate with NASA.

Final selfie from April 2022

GLOSSARY

asteroid
Small, rocky object that orbits the Sun

Asteroid Belt
Huge, ring-shaped area of the Solar System, located between Mars and Jupiter, and home to thousands of asteroids

astronaut
Person who travels into space

astronomer
Person who studies space

astrophysicist
Person who studies the structure of stars, planets, and other space objects

atmosphere
Layer of gases that surrounds a planet or moon

aurora
Lights that appear in the sky above the polar regions of Earth and other planets

axis
Imaginary line that passes through the centre of a planet or star, around which the planet or star rotates

celestial object
Natural object located outside Earth's atmosphere, such as a star, planet, or moon

climate
Average weather conditions of an area

comet
Object made of ice and dust that orbits the Sun, developing a tail when it is close to the Sun

crater
Dip in the surface of a planet or other solid object in the Solar System, caused by an object crashing into it

eclipse
When an object is in the shadow of another object

ESA
European Space Agency, an agency dedicated to the exploration of space

exoplanet
Planet orbiting a star that is not in our Solar System

farside
Side of the Moon that can't be seen from Earth

fusion
Process that combines two or more things

galaxy
Large collection of stars, dust, gas, and space, held together by gravity

gas giant
Large planet that is mostly made of gas, such as Jupiter

geology
The study of the ground and rocks on planets

gravity
Invisible force that is caused by mass, which pulls objects towards each other

ice giant
Large planet that is mostly made of gas with a layer of ice, such as Uranus

infrared
A type of light with a longer wavelength than visible light

ISS
International Space Station, an orbiting laboratory used for scientific and space research

Kuiper Belt
Part of the Solar System beyond the planet Neptune, which contains small, frozen objects

lander
Spacecraft designed to land on a moon or a planet

lunar
Relating to the Moon

mass
Measurement of how much matter is in an object

matter
Substance that has mass and takes up space

meteor
When a meteoroid burns up as it enters Earth's atmosphere, appearing as a streak of light

meteorite
The remains of a meteor that lands on the surface of a planet or moon

meteoroid
Small piece of an asteroid or comet in space

Milky Way
Our galaxy

Moon
Natural object made of rock, or rock and ice, which orbits a planet or asteroid

NASA
National Aeronautics and Space Administration, a US agency dedicated to the study of space science

nearside
Side of the Moon that can be seen from Earth

nebula
Cloud of gas and dust floating in space

Oort Cloud
The huge collection of icy objects that is believed to surround the Solar System

orbit
Path a celestial object takes around another due to gravity, such as the path planets travel around the Sun

planet
Large, spherical object that orbits a star

probe
Uncrewed spacecraft designed to study objects in space and send information back to Earth

radar
Technology that detects far-away objects by sending out radio waves, which bounce off the object back to the radar

rover
Uncrewed vehicle for exploring the surface of a planet or moon

satellite
Object that orbits another larger object. It can be natural, such as rock, or artifical

solar panel
Panel that uses solar cells to create electricity from the energy in sunlight

Solar System
Collection of objects that orbit the Sun, including planets, moons, asteroids, and comets

spacecraft
Vehicle that travels in space

star
Huge, glowing sphere of gas, such as the Sun

telescope
Tool used to look at objects very far away

Universe
Place that is home to everything humanity knows of

Index

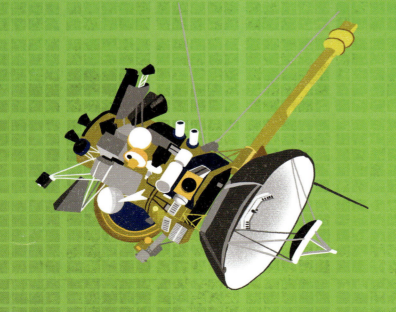

ACKNOWLEDGEMENTS

DK would like to thank Laura Gilbert for the index; Polly Goodman for proofreading; Anna Bonnerjea, Robin Moul, and Dawn Sirett for additional editing; and Eleanor Bates, Ann Cannings, and Sif Nørskov for design assistance. Special thanks to Sophie Allan and Josh Barker at the UK National Space Academy for their endless enthusiasm and expertise.

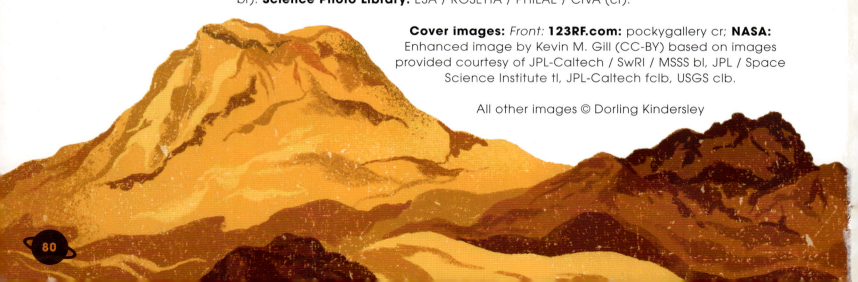